This is the story of Noah

and the ark

and the rainbow.

It's in the Bible in the Book of Genesis for everyone to read.

You know God always brings good to people.
But in the days of Noah,
    many bad things were happening.
That's because most people
    didn't pay any attention to God.
But Noah listened to God. He was fair to everyone,
    and he acted just the way he ought to act.
The Bible says Noah walked with God.

Noah had a wife and three sons.
His sons were Shem and Ham and Japheth,
   and they had wives, too.
One day God told Noah,
"Bad things are happening on the earth.
They'll have to stop.
Because so many people are being wicked
   there's going to be a big flood.

It's going to rain forty days and forty nights.
It's going to rain so much that
 water will cover the whole earth.
Every wicked thing will be
 washed away by the water.

But you, Noah, have listened to me.
You've been good.
Now, do exactly what I tell you to do.
Then you and your family will be safe."
Noah did exactly what God told him to do.

He built an enormous ark.

He built three closed-in decks on the ark—

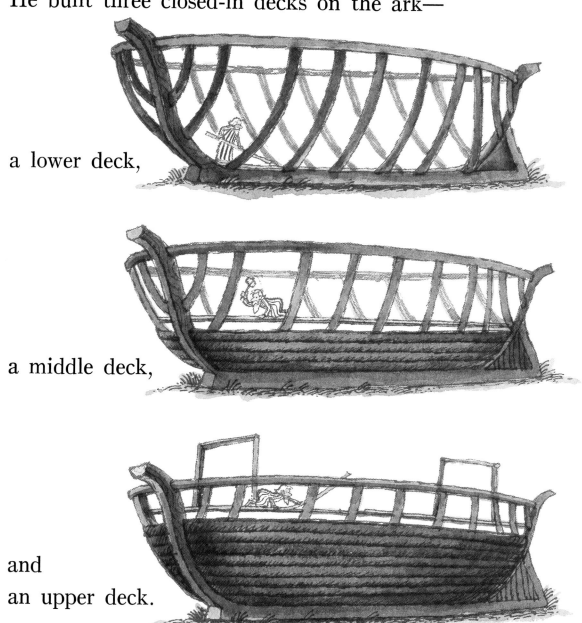

a lower deck,

a middle deck,

and
an upper deck.

He made rooms inside. He made a door in the side

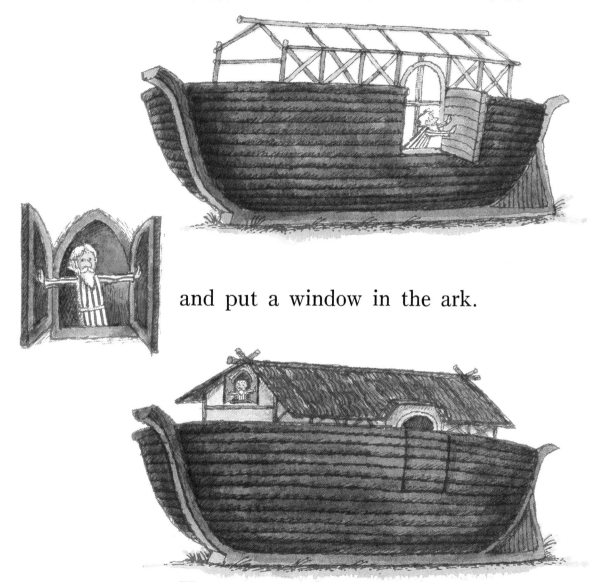

and put a window in the ark.

He put a roof on top.

He covered the inside and outside with tar
 to keep out water.

When he had finished all the work,
 Noah took his wife
 and his sons, Shem and Ham and Japheth,
 and their wives, into the ark.

God told Noah, "Take a male and female
   of every kind of animal and bird into the ark, too,
   and a male and female of every kind of reptile."

Noah did.

He took apes and badgers and bears and boars,
hippos and foxes and goats and sheep,
leopards and lions and moles and mice,
hyenas and horses and jackals and pigs,
camels and cattle and weasels and wolves,
deer and elephants, dogs and cats.

He took eagles and sparrows and ravens and owls,
vultures and chickens and swallows and bats,
swans and pelicans and peacocks and storks,
ostriches, falcons and pigeons and doves.

He took lizards and turtles and snakes and worms,
caterpillars, ants and bees and beetles,
and flies and locusts and fleas,

and many, many, many,
more.

And Noah took some of every kind of food
so not a single creature in the ark would be hungry.

Well, not many days after Noah finished
getting all the creatures and food into the ark
it began to rain.

It rained,

and it **rained**,

and it **rained**,

and it **rained,**

just as God had said it would.

First the water covered the ground.

Then it covered the trees and the little hills.

Then it crept up the mountains

until it covered the tops of even the highest mountains.

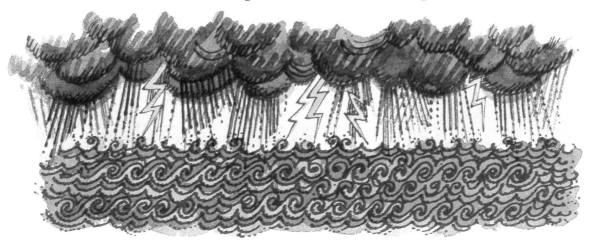

It rained forty days and forty nights.
Everything was covered with water.
But the ark floated easily and smoothly
   on top of the water.

And Noah and his family,
   and all the creatures inside the ark,
   were dry and snug and safe.

Even after the rain stopped,
   the water covered the earth for months.

Then the wind began to blow,
  and little by little the water went down.

At last the ark came to rest
  on the mountain of Ararat.

Soon after that, Noah looked out the window
  and he could see the tops of the mountains.

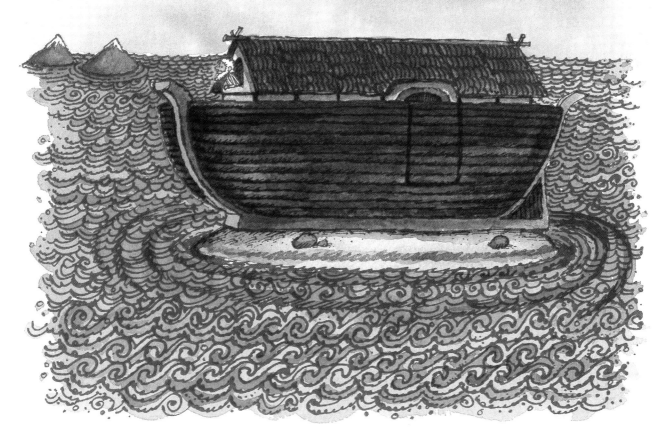

The water kept going down,

and down,

and down,

So pretty soon Noah opened the window
and sent out a dove.

The dove flew around for a little while.

When she couldn't find a dry place to perch,
she came back to the ark.
Noah put out his hand and took her in.

A week later Noah sent out the dove again.
This time she was gone all day.
When she came back to the ark that evening,
she held a fresh olive branch in her beak.

"Hmmm," said Noah.
"The water must be almost gone.
At least it isn't higher than
   the olive trees anymore."

He waited still another week,
   and sent the dove out again.
This time the dove didn't come back.
So Noah knew she had found a dry place to rest.

Now, Noah lifted up the roof of the ark
   and looked all around.

The earth was dry again!

"All right, Noah," God said.
"You can come out of the ark now.
And bring with you your wife
   and your sons and their wives,
   and all those creatures
   you took into the ark."

So Noah and his wife,
   and his sons and their wives,

and all the walking, creeping, crawling, flying creatures
that had been living in the ark all those months
came out of the ark, safe and sound.

Out came the apes and badgers and bears and boars,
hippos and foxes and goats and sheep,
leopards and lions and moles and mice,
hyenas and horses and jackals and pigs,
camels and cattle and weasels and wolves,
deer and elephants, dogs and cats.

 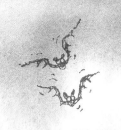

Out came the eagles and sparrows and ravens and owls,
vultures and chickens and swallows and bats,
swans and pelicans, peacocks and storks,
ostriches, falcons and pigeons and doves.
Out came the lizards and turtles and snakes and worms,
caterpillars, and ants and bees and beetles,
and flies and locusts and fleas,

and many, many, many, more.

And God told Noah,
"Whenever you see a rainbow in the sky,
  remember that I'm always keeping you safe."

Now, we don't have to wait for a rainbow
  to help us remember, do we?
We can always know that listening to God,
  and walking with God,
  keeps us safe —
  just as it kept Noah
  and his family
  and all the animals
  in the ark
  safe and sound.